# NO TWO ARE ALIKE

# NO TWO ARE ALIKE

## A MEMOIR OF FAITH, FAMILY, AND ENCOUNTERING GOD

CAROLINE CORRIGAN O'NEAL

NEW DEGREE PRESS

NO TWO ARE ALIKE
*A Memoir of Faith, Family, and Encountering God*

ISBN    978-1-64137-465-1  *Paperback*
        978-1-64137-466-8  *Kindle Ebook*
        978-1-64137-467-5  *Ebook*

*These dedications hold such dear places in my heart. First and foremost, I want to dedicate this book to God. Thank you for giving me this opportunity to share my story.*

*I also want to say thank you to my family for all the prayers and support with this book. They mean the world to me! I want to say thank you especially to my mom for creating a school that has changed my life forever! Thank you for accepting God's will and living out the plan He had for your life. Because of this place, I am a new and changed person, and I now see God the way I was meant to see Him all along. I see myself in a whole new light, and I can share with others who they are made to be in Him.*

*For my twin sister, Claire: I miss you every day and think of you always.*

*For my husband, Chris: Thank you for being the man you are. Your prayers and support mean a lot to me!*

*For my Papa, Grandma, and Grandpa: May you always live on in spirit.*

*Thank you also to everyone at Sophia Academy who made it the place it was. This school would not have been what it was without you.*

# CONTENTS

# SPECIAL ACKNOWLEDGMENTS

———

God
Vic and Marie Corrigan
Charlie and Louise Loudermilk
Paul, Mellie, and James Napolitano
Victor and Mary Claire Corrigan
Chris O'Neal
Liza O'Neal
Frank and Laura Corrigan
Frank and Alden Corrigan
Kevin and Delia Corrigan
Tom and Eileen Jones
Bill and Lynne Yarbrough
Paul and Joelle Yarbrough
Dorothy Smith
Louis Corrigan
Mimi Abrams
Jenny Alms
Ken and Cathi Athaide
Ginny Balkcom
Steve and Nancy Balkcom

Stacy Bean
Brian Bies
Tom and Anne Boshinski
John and Elizabeth Bresnahan and Family
Jack and Elizabeth Brown
Carlton Byrd
Mike Chambers
Beth Chandler
Amy Codman
Tom and Kathy Cotney
Kathryn Crabtree
Anne Foster
Kate Foster
Linda Goodman
Elissa Graeser
Lynda Guthrie
Kim Hanna
Father John Harhager
Jeanne Heekin
Renee Houle
Grace Izard
Andrew and Elizabeth King
Eric Koester
Bishop Joel Konzen, SM
Lynn Lanier
Melissa Lappe
Coley Loudermilk
Robin and Frances Loudermilk
Father David Musso
John Napolitano
Mark and Mary Anne Napolitano
Sara Neel

Elina Oliferovskiy

Joan Walker Page

Jenny Papevies

Gjorgji Pejkovski

Sant and Shawn Perez

Anthony and Angela Randazzo

Toni Rhett

Zane Rhoades and Robert Raiford

Pat Riddle

Lisa Robinson

Father Bill Rowland, SM

Jody Sams

Ruthanna Schofield

Gayle Sherlag

Laura Smith

John and Mildred Spalding

Kathleen Swann

Jim & Mary Tapp

Ginia Taylor

Carrie Thompson

John Turner

Thank you so much to everyone who contributed to my book journey. I apologize if I missed your name.

# FOREWORD BY MARIE CORRIGAN

Within these pages my precious daughter, Caroline, has bared her heart and soul about being a person with a learning difference. Beautiful on the outside, with no physical signs of being someone who needs time to process, to understand, to form a response and to release that response, she has often, most of the time, been a quiet observer. While being a quiet observer, she has not felt the comfort and inclusion into the group who moves faster with their processing and responses. Instead, she has used her consequences of an extremely premature birth and numerous health challenges to develop deep and profound relationships with her family and her faith, both of which have sustained her throughout her life. These have reassured her of her value and meaningfulness in a world that can be harshly critical and demanding. Caroline has managed these situations with courage and grace. As I've told her and her siblings many times, Caroline has more courage than anyone I have ever met.

Starting a school for students with learning differences was not easy, but it was absolutely the right thing to do for Caroline. Her dad and I were not going to let her flounder and fail in institutions of learning that cared so little and did the least for the students that needed the most. What we wanted for her, and what she wanted, was a place that emulated the schools her siblings attended: a faith-based school with a complete curriculum and extracurricular activities, teachers and staff who were committed to the mission, and a belief in each student—that they were perfect in God's sight and had much to accomplish if given the opportunity. We had so many success stories, and for me, the greatest success was to see Caroline not just survive school but to thrive!

Completing college, cum laude, entering the workforce, and marrying her soulmate have been the blessings for all the years of trials and tears, being left out and left behind, and the fears of all the unknowns.

Still the beautiful, petite girl, still a quiet observer, still fortified by her family and faith—there's still so much that she'll accomplish. I often think of what a joy it would be to go back to all the naysayers who were quick to put limits on what her progress and outcomes would be. Don't believe all the negative things you may hear about your child. Keep moving forward, one step at a time. Hold tightly to your child, encouraging them continuously, and remember that God is in control—always.

Caroline, we're so proud of you! And we're so blessed that God sent you to us!

I love you,

Mom

# INTRODUCTION

―――――

While I was working on a certain class assignment, I started feeling very nervous and restless. It was as if I could tell someone was watching me to make sure I was doing everything right the way I was supposed to and not messing up for one second. When I began my assignment, I had my eyes glued to the paper as if someone would snatch the paper out of my hands. I focused my attention on my paper and pencil, my eyes so intent on the blank page. As I was filling out answers one by one, I heard voices in my head telling me, "Caroline, you will be the last one. You will not finish on time. You won't get this assignment written."

At the time, I didn't know this voice was the enemy, but it was. While writing, I could feel my breath getting louder and louder, heavier and heavier. All of a sudden, I started feeling tears in my eyes from how much pressure I was putting on myself to make sure I was perfect.

No one is perfect.

My name is Caroline O'Neal. I live in Atlanta, Georgia, with my husband, Chris. I was born three months early. Since I was born prematurely, my parents were advised to be aware of the potential of a learning difference due to my low birth weight and extreme prematurity. The learning difference I have is called auditory processing disorder. At the time of my birth, my lungs lacked adequate surfactant, which is the substance naturally produced in the third trimester to keep the lungs from sticking together. There is a drug that treats this condition; it is administered to premature babies to aid their lung development. Unfortunately for me, this drug was being used in a trial study at another major hospital in Atlanta, and it had not received FDA approval yet. Most of the babies born as early as I was at the other hospital received this medication and fared much better with their lung function. I, on the other hand, would need oxygen twenty-four hours a day for six-and-a-half years, and for the first few years afterward, the oxygen tank traveled wherever I went just in case I needed it. I do consider myself fortunate, though, because my pulmonologist thought I would never be able to live without supplemental oxygen.

Another cause for worry was my eyes, since many premature babies suffer from permanent eye conditions and blindness. Thankfully, I was not one of them. Another challenge for me was eating; feeding me would take hours because I would get so tired from trying to eat. When I did finish a bottle, as soon as my parents burped me, it would all come back up and the entire process would have to start over again. Feeding me took hours and hours a day.

When I was in fourth grade, I attended a private school. Each day, students and I in each class would receive pennies that would be laid on the top of our desks, taped to the desks so they would not fall off. We would receive these pennies if we completed our work or did a good job on assignments or homework. We would get them taken away if we did not turn in homework or did not complete assignments. At the end of each week, our homeroom teacher would allow us to buy a toy, whichever toy we wanted, from the class treasure chest, but only if we had all five pennies on our desks.

I remember one Friday, I was sitting at my desk and counting to see how many pennies I had. I had a total of four pennies. You know what that meant? I wanted that penny. I was going to do just about anything to get that penny. It was all I could focus on in that moment. I was very excited about receiving this last penny to get a gift at the end of the week. My teacher gave us a written assignment to work on that day. The assignment we were given was to complete a fill-in-the-blank assignment to finish the rest of sentences. Even though this classwork assignment was not timed, I felt as if it was. In other words, I was afraid that, yet again, I would be the last one to finish and all the students would be finished before me. The teachers in my classes told us when we started, as they had told us many times, that this was not a race. They wanted us to take our time to make sure we understood everything and to ask questions if we needed help.

At one point, when feeling nervous and stressed, I felt no choice but to look away from my sheet. When I saw my teacher at her desk, she gave me a smile. She asked me if I was okay and if I needed help or had questions. I said no because I was afraid if I did ask for help, I would start crying and make a fool of myself. All my life, because of my learning difference, I put pressure on myself to have excellent and top performance. If I didn't, I considered myself a failure. Every area in my life, especially in school, made me want to identify as a perfect person. What is the definition of perfect? The word "perfect" means no mistakes. The learning difference I have, or the fact that I was born with one, has made me feel this pressure to make no mistakes. Due to my learning difference, I thought God was punishing or cursing me.

When I was finished with my sheet, I got up from my desk and walked over to my teacher's desk to give it to her. As she was scanning it, I started thinking thoughts like, "I hope I didn't mess up at all, did not make any mistakes, and got every answer right." When she finished checking it, she looked at me and told me I did a very good job and I got every answer right. She gave me my fifth penny. Because of that fifth penny, I was able to get a toy from the treasure chest. I felt like I was on cloud nine. I was so happy!

Looking back at the way I used to feel about myself then compared to the way I feel about myself now, I see things have dramatically changed. From defining and identifying myself as a girl with a learning difference to how I see myself now, my thoughts and mindset have changed. I have taken a 180-degree turn. Throughout my life, God has shown me and taught me, through people and Himself, that according to Him I can do all things through Christ who strengthens me. He has told me, through Himself and people, that a learning difference does not define me unless I let it. This is not my identity. I can still do all things through Him who strengthens me. I am much improved because of the transformation of my mindset. Though it took many years for this new mindset to come about, and for the change in the way I see myself to the way God sees me, I would not change the past. According to how God sees me and what He says about me, I have nothing wrong with me and never have. Throughout my life and what I have been through, God has brought me closer to Him and allowed me to have a personal relationship with Him. A relationship with God, my Father in Heaven, whom I love dearly and who loves me is all that matters.

Yet for years, I felt like I had to teach myself in school to be a "good girl," or rather, a "perfect person." I cannot tell you how relieved I was when I met others who also have learning differences. I have told many people I do understand what it's like to be alone. I do understand how it feels to be the only one left out or like you are the only person in the world who feels this way. In addition, I understand how it feels to think you are less than a person or don't measure up simply because your brain is wired differently. I know how frustrating it can be when you've studied for many hours, and it feels like forever, only to forget information just because your brain processes and remembers it differently. Even if you feel this way, it doesn't mean you are not good enough.

God is saying to you, even though you have a learning difference, you are still good enough; you are enough as a person because He made you. You are made in His image. We are all made in the image of God.

I decided to write this book for many reasons. God laid this on my heart and told me both through Himself and other people to write it. I felt and knew in my heart that this story needed to be told. This story is about Sophia Academy, a school that my mom founded for me and for other children with learning differences. I believe this story needed to be written and told most of all to show who God is and His love for everyone. Sophia Academy will always hold a special place in my heart. The school has always been a second home to me and will forever be one. The school was a place where I could come to be myself when I didn't feel I could be anywhere else. Sophia Academy was a place of warmth, care, kindness, positivity, enthusiasm, and, most importantly, love. Sophia Academy was Heaven on earth. When I was at Sophia Academy, I always felt the presence of God—whether I was with my mom, teachers, students, or just in the building. At

Sophia Academy, everyone was loved for who they are and accepted for who they are.

Today, I am thankful for my learning difference. Over time, God has taught me and showed me how my learning difference has brought me closer to Him. No, my brain doesn't work the same way as everyone else's, but everyone's brains are different—that is how God created them. He created everyone to be unique and to be different. Whatever your weaknesses are, God works in the biggest ways. Your worth and value are not in your learning difference, nor will they ever be. Your worth and value, as well as who you are as a person, are in Him. We all are different in one way or another; that makes us special and unique as people. God made us different on purpose. He wants us to be who He has called us to be.

For all the years I was at Sophia Academy, I felt and believed nothing was wrong with me. I had no restrictions or limitations on myself. It was as if, even though I knew this place was a school for kids with learning differences, this was the right place for me. Even though I knew this place was a school for children with learning differences, I didn't see it that way. Don't get me wrong, no one wants to be "so special" that they need to go to a special school, but—in my experience—this is the only way to get the correct for students with learning differences. However, this didn't matter to me at all. It didn't matter because I never put my focus on people's learning styles. I never noticed other people's worries, struggles, or obstacles because I focused on God. He does not want me or for anyone to worry because doing so won't add any minutes to our lives. He only wants people to focus on Him.

At Sophia Academy, God's presence filled the school, and being inside the school made me feel very connected to God. He wanted me, along with everyone else, to feel this way, to feel safe. Being part of a lower student-to-teacher ratio, I felt more at ease, and I could understand the information better. I felt accepted, and when I needed one-on-one instruction, it was no big deal. I felt calmer and happier learning this way.

This book is for people with learning differences, parents of children with learning differences, people of all or any faiths or of no faith. This book is also for people who want to know about God and who He is.

Within these pages, you'll learn more about me and understand a Father's love for His child and see Him working through my parents, family, and school. This book will show God working through my parents to overcome any obstacles to help their daughter have the best education possible, and one that fit her needs. This book will also show how we can experience faith, love, and hope with God's help and trust in Him. With God, all things are possible!

## CHAPTER ONE

# FAITH, FAMILY, AND MYSELF

When I was a little girl, within my family, I was a happy and friendly child. I would also describe myself as quiet, reserved, and shy with those I did not know. If in my safe environment, I would no longer see myself as a quiet and shy person or someone with a learning difference.

My parents' names are Vic and Marie Corrigan. I am the eldest of four siblings, and their names are Louise, Mellie, and Victor. My family and I are very close with each other. Many words come to mind when I think of my family, but the first word that comes to mind is "faith."

However, I was not always this way with my faith. In fact, I was indifferent to faith. Maybe it was because I did not understand what it meant to be a Christian or a Catholic, but I thought so often, "How is it possible to have your faith be an important part of your life? How is it possible to have a relationship with God?" Deep in my heart, I wanted something more. I wanted to know who God was, I wanted to dive deep into my faith, and most of all, I wanted a personal relationship with Him and be my true self the way He created me to be. I did not know how this would happen, but some way I hoped it would.

My parents have always demonstrated who God is, and they made it very important through their actions, manner, and speech—everything they did was to teach us about Him and the Catholic faith. I have countless memories of us sitting at dinner or having conversations with each other where my parents would recite stories from the Bible, even though we had heard them on numerous occasions.

We would attend Sunday Mass, as well as Mass on any days that were considered holy days of obligation, as a family at our home parish in Atlanta. Holy days of obligation are certain days where members of the Catholic faith attend Mass; these days include Christmas, Ascension of Mary, and All Saints' Day. Since I did not attend Catholic school when my siblings did, my parents had to put me in Sunday school at our home parish. I hated Sunday school! I was totally unfamiliar with the building, and I didn't know any of the other students or the teachers. Each week, I would go through the same process, trying to find the room I was supposed to be in and trying to become comfortable with everyone in the class. It was so stressful! My mother finally asked the director of the program if she could home school me on the information, and that's how I got credit for going through the Catholic formation classes.

When we lived in my parents' house growing up, my parents would tell my siblings and me before Sunday approached that we would be attending Mass. Every Sunday morning, my parents would come into each of our rooms, one by one, to wake us up. When my mom came into our room, she would walk over to our bed and whisper to us that it was time to wake up. My dad, on the other hand, would walk into our room, turn on the light, and say, "Good morning! You need to get up and get ready for Mass!" My parents insisted we have a good foundation in our Catholic faith; they were bringing us up in the tradition of the faith and, most importantly, to know who God is.

Learning about God and the Catholic faith, I did not understand these two areas of life. I did not know why I needed to know who God was, much less have a relationship with Him. I did not know that much about the Catholic faith, except for listening to homilies, praying in Mass, praying at dinner with my family, and saying the Our Father and Hail Mary. Even to this day, my parents often tell us to treat people the way God would treat us, including ourselves. They would tell us to love people exactly the way God wanted us to love them.

My parents did a great job being godly role models for us by praying for us and guiding us closer to God with our faith. They are very kind, generous, giving, and loving people, exemplifying God in many ways. Every morning and night, they prayed for us. They wanted us all to have a strong faith and relationship with God and carry that out in our lives. Working together to build a strong foundation for these qualities in their home, they made it very important for us to have faith in our lives. I am very thankful to have parents who love my siblings and me as much as they do. My parents show love to us in many ways, and the love they show us is the way God shows His love to us.

From my former relationship with God to my relationship with Him today, God matured me greatly and changed me from not wanting to know about Him to falling in love with Him. I wanted to know the truth to many unanswered questions—such as who I am and what is my purpose. Every question I asked Him, He has answered. I have dived deeper into my Catholic faith. I have a sense of peace and purpose, and I hope for that for everyone.

## CHAPTER TWO

# LIFE BEFORE SOPHIA ACADEMY

---

I had few options regarding starting school. This was because, even though I was not using oxygen, my pulmonologist insisted an oxygen tank be onsite and available to me in the event I had a respiratory crisis. By federal law, public schools must take all students regardless of their issues. This settled the question; I would be starting school at the neighborhood public school. This school was known to be one of the best in Atlanta. Most public schools at that time did not have specific learning environments for a student like me.

Each morning, when getting ready for the day, I would dread going to school. When my mom would drop me off at school, I would either be crying or stay quiet in the car and begin crying when she dropped me off. I felt so embarrassed whenever people saw me crying. Not only would I get stares from them, but people asked me why my face was red and what was wrong. I cried every day in school because I felt lost and overwhelmed. Everything was too much for me to handle. The people, the classes, the cafeteria—everything was so big! In my classes, I found it very hard to be a student. Additionally, I didn't feel part of the school community. Everyone else seemed to have friends, but I had no one.

Even though I did not know I had a learning difference, my parents had given the administration and my teacher documentation to support my diagnosis and the type of instruction I needed. My kindergarten and first grade teachers totally ignored all the documentation. Everyone in the room got the same instruction no matter what. In second grade, I could tell my teacher wanted to help me. She seemed to understand my learning issues, and she worked hard to give me extra support. But so many students were in the classroom, and I understand now that many others, just like me, needed more individualized and specific instruction. When I worked on my assignments, I would either be behind because I could not understand what I needed to do, or the assignment was too long for the time allowed. Every day, I was frustrated and unhappy about the situation.

I did enjoy computer class because it was a smaller student-to-teacher ratio. I was relieved to have the focus and attention on me, which meant I could receive the help I needed. Little did I know that technology, specifically assistive technology, would be the key to my academic success in the future.

One day, I was the only one still working on a worksheet in class—all of the other students left to play outside during recess. I wanted to play outside as well, but my teacher told me a few minutes prior to recess that I would have to stay inside to finish my work. I became very sad and quiet when I heard this. As I sat at my desk, I watched each student, one by one, leave the classroom. It was only me and the teacher in the room. When the last student left the room, I turned around and stared at my worksheet. I became very unhappy.

Tears started streaming down my face as I tried to work on my worksheet. My teacher was sitting next to me, watching me as I worked. She noticed I was silent and asked me what was wrong. As my eyes started filling up with more tears, I asked, "Why am I always the last one?" I did not understand why this kept happening. I do not remember what my teacher said to me in that moment, but I do remember she gave me a hug. The hug was very warm and affectionate, and I felt better when I hugged her. I kept working on my worksheet after that, but it didn't make it easier to come to terms with being the only one who was asked to stay behind and finish her work while everyone else could play.

Even with these positives, my overall experience with public school was negative. The building, the classes, and everything about the school was daunting. I never had my needs met the way I needed and wanted. I never had the opportunity for success.

One thing attending public school did show me and my parents was the gross lack of resources and support offered to students who have learning differences despite any amount of supported documentation, conferences with the teachers and administration, and actually bringing in outside experts in this field to champion our cases. Due to the school's inability and lack of desire to support my learning style, my parents found a private school more suited to my learning needs.

Eventually, I left the public school system. I was thrilled! I attended private school for second through fourth grade. This school was initially located in North Sandy Springs. It was only fifteen miles away, but due to Atlanta traffic, the drive could take one hour to an hour and a half. Every day, my mom had to drive my siblings to their school and then start the long drive to my school. When my siblings arrived at their school, I would get so sad. They all got to be together, and I wanted to be with them. I wanted so badly to go to the same school.

This particular private school was very small and was housed in a permanent trailer behind a church—what a different look from the school my siblings attended. But I was content because I felt comfortable here and supported as a student.

From the day I entered the school doors until the time I left to go home, I was reminded throughout the day that I had a learning difference. The teaching style was different, the curriculum was different, the amount of work was different, and the amount of time allowed to get the assignments finished was different. Given this environment, I wanted to do my best. I would spend many hours on anything I was given just to make sure it had no mistakes. I didn't realize how much pressure I was putting on myself.

To make matters worse, I did not feel accepted at this school the way I wanted to be. I'm very petite, typically very quiet, and tend to be a loner, although I wanted to be a part of the group. What I craved was acceptance from people. I was accepted by my teachers and the principal, but not by the students. In fact, I was bullied. I was bullied because I was so shy and I was small for my age. People didn't take me seriously. Every day, I felt worse and worse about myself. These negative feelings had me in turmoil. I felt very excluded, which caused me to go further into my shell. I began to have this worry of what people would say and think about me.

One of the memories that comes to mind is when I was in the girl's restroom. Two students were in there with me. I could hear them talking with each other. They did not notice I was in the stall as I was as quiet as a mouse, making sure they didn't hear me breathe. Seconds later, they had turned the lights out—and there I was, standing in the bathroom stall, alone. I was terrified. Since I did not have a light to find my way out, I found there to be no choice but to scream as loud as I could. I stayed in the stall for thirty to forty-five minutes. While standing in the bathroom stall, I started praying and saying, "God, please help me! I'm so scared!" Over and over, I kept repeating the same sentences. I was also crying at this point. After many minutes standing in the stall screaming, I heard the same students who were in the bathroom before walk in and turn on the light. "Caroline, are you in here?" one of the students asked. I was so embarrassed she would hear the noise of me sniffing and whimpering from crying. "Yes, I am. I am in the bathroom stall." I then walked out of the stall, tears running down my face, I looked terrible! She then told me our teacher was looking for me. I started walking back to the building with them. I saw them both laughing with each other. I asked them, "What's so funny?" They replied, "Oh, nothing, don't worry about it!" And then went back to laughing. Without them telling me, I could sense they were laughing at me and the scene of me crying from being so scared. When my teacher saw me, she was so relieved I was safe.

Another memory I have is when I was outside with my Beanie Babies. One day, I took them to school to keep me company throughout the day. I referred to them as my best friends. As I was walking by the basketball hoop, one of the students asked me if he could have my Beanie Babies. Without giving me time to say yes, he grabbed them from me and started throwing each of them one by one in the air through the hoop, hoping the hoop would catch them and the Beanie Babies would stay there. As I watched him, I screamed, "Please stop, please! Don't do that, those are mine!" He ignored me and didn't even care that he was bullying me. I was enraged at him for practically grabbing my stuffed animals out of my hands and taking them as if they were his. I was so furious that I ran back inside to tell my teacher what he had done. I do not remember exactly what happened after this, but I do remember staying inside the classroom because of how upset I was.

There was also a specific performance the students had to conduct one night at the school. Since the chapel was located in another building, we had to walk to this building to get to the chapel. I was excited but anxious about this event. We had to discuss something specific, I think about a president or something similar. I was next in line as some of the students went before me reciting their speeches, and I was very nervous. I started feeling a knot in my throat, followed by my body heating up on the inside and outside. As I walked up to the microphone, my voice began to quiver when I was about to speak the words. I couldn't help but cry. I just stood there, crying while holding my sheet. I was humiliated! My teacher, feeling awful for me, walked up to me, hugged me, and said, "It's okay, come along." The other students began laughing at me making a fool out of myself. As I sat down in the back with the other students, my teacher said my speech for me. She did a very good job, and I was thankful not to have that embarrassment on me anymore and so grateful she had come to the rescue to save me from the humiliation I had experienced.

As a result, I began to struggle with my sense of self-worth. I did not know who I was anymore. Day by day, as the students treated me the way they did, I started accepting this was who I was and the negative words they said about me were true. These lies that the enemy had used as a way to steal my joy and my true self were totally detrimental. All the while, the more the enemy was pushing me further into the lies, God was pulling me out of them. In the depths of my heart, in those quiet moments, God would whisper to me, "You are made for more! This is not who you are!" Through teachers, my parents, and my siblings, I could see God was speaking to me, telling me the truth of who I was.

The only people I believed accepted me were my teacher and my principal. I could tell they generally accepted me for the person I was, inside and out. Many days, I even wished my teachers and my principal were the same age as me so we could be best friends.

When I was attending this school, I did not think this was any better from the last school experience I had. At the private school, I felt that terrible feeling of nobody accepting me for who I was and no one wanting to get to know me for the person I was, and that took away from any positives I might have encountered.

Many times, I would feel this way or think this way about school, myself, and my life, and I wanted this feeling to go away. I wanted the feeling of loneliness and friendless-ness—with no way for me to feel or be myself—to all go away. I did not know when or how I would stop feeling this way or what would be the next step, but I *knew* this would stop. I knew I could love school in all the ways a child has always wanted to, and that there was a road to a better life.

Although I did not yet know how, an amazing change was coming sooner than I expected. I was excited to experience this! I had a feeling my next move would be a much bigger and better plan for my life than I could ever have imagined or dreamed of. I knew everything was happening for a reason, that I was experiencing these feelings and being treated this way for a specific reason.

God knew exactly what would happen next in my life, and He wanted this for me as much as I wanted it myself.

## CHAPTER THREE

# FROM CONCEPTION TO DELIVERY

———

My parents were very worried about where I would attend school. They did not have ideas in mind or know where to place me in school. My parents consistently prayed every day for an answer from God, hoping He would tell them what He wanted them to do. They attended Mass whenever they could, prayed the rosary, read their Bible, and prayed together daily. My parents were emotionally, physically, and spiritually drained and wanted an answer to their problem. They wanted a faith-based school, a school like my siblings attended, just for me. My mom called out to God, "I'll do anything if you just give me the answer." With those words, everything changed!

When my mom was praying and asking God for the answer, He spoke to her in her heart, telling her, "Marie, I want you to start a school." Stunned and shocked, she thought, "Start a school? What? You're kidding, right?" She did not like the answer she heard. She did not want to do what God was telling her to do because she thought this was too much for her to handle. She had four children, aged four through nine. However, praying, hoping for a new answer or hoping for a new idea, she would always be led back to this answer. In a clear, strong voice, He reminded her of her bargain: "I'll do anything if you just get me out of this." When she agreed to this command, God was then able to give her the tools to start this school. My mom realized *she* was the solution to the problem. God provided her with the direction she needed; she would start a school similar to the private school I had attended. Ideas began to swirl around in her head continuously. My mom, still reluctant to start a school, knew this was the solution that was needed for me. She knew, after putting the pieces together, that this would be the only fit for me and the only way I would ever feel happy in a school and get the right education I needed. Even though she thought this was too big for her to manage, it was not too big for God. In fact, nothing is too big for Him to handle! The idea was conceived, and now it was time to bring it to delivery.

Sophia Academy would be a unique school for unique learners. This school would be for children of average to superior IQ scores who did not do well in a traditional environment. It was intended for children who had similar learning differences of processing or attention deficits or dyslexia. This school would have small classes, multi-sensory instruction, and a specific language program. Most importantly, it would be a Christian school.

Now that she knew what to do, the next obstacle was to face my dad. She did not know what his reaction would be to this, but she knew she had to tell him. She was nervous about telling him because of the way he might respond. She knew she had to tell him so they could come to an agreement about working as a team to make this idea come to life. "Vic,

God wants me to start a school for Caroline and children with learning differences."

Stunned, my dad was initially angry. "Marie, have you lost your mind? May I remind you that you have a nursing degree, not an education degree? You also have four children to take care of. My job is very demanding. If you start a school, who is going to take care of everything else? Who is going to take care of me?" All the while, even though he was angry, he was also frustrated, desperate, and very concerned about my education. God had my dad right where He wanted him. He had both of my parents right where He wanted them.

My mom felt daunted and frightened about this undertaking God wanted her to make. To make this easier on my mom, she decided to ignore what God was telling her. She thought it would be best to first take the route of incorporating a program for students with learning differences into an established Catholic school. She truly believed she was on the right track. She felt really good about everything.

Even though she was scared about pursuing this, she felt God was with her every step of the way, giving her direction. When my mom felt scared, she would pray for God to take her fear away and replace it with energy and enthusiasm needed to meet the goal. She asked to meet with the archbishop of Atlanta and managed to arrange a meeting with him. She was excited and was looking forward to the meeting. When she told my dad she was going to meet with the archbishop, he went ballistic! My dad said, "How can you do this? You are not even an educator!" However, he cleared his calendar and made sure he could attend the meeting with her.

When they met with the archbishop, he was very patient and attentive. The archbishop said, "You have a good idea, and we will not stand in your way." There it was! He had given his approval. However, when my mom walked to the parking lot after the meeting was over, she realized the archbishop had not approved these classes to be added to the Catholic education system. This mission was not going to happen, at least not at this time, in a Catholic school.

My mom felt as if she was failing God at this point. She was starting to realize this was not the plan God wanted. She believed this was God's plan for her; however, she was so discouraged with the progress she had made. She wanted God to give her guidance and told God that if this was not His plan, she would accept it and do what He wanted her to do.

During the next few months, my mom felt like she had two completely separate brains. One brain was the everyday brain that handled her children, her husband, and the house. The second brain constantly visualized the creation of the school. She was possessed by these thoughts and could not stop them. Whispers from Heaven were always in the back of her brain.

My mom's dream was for Sophia Academy be a Catholic school. However, this was not God's plan—not yet, at least. After my mom met with the archbishop, she received a call from someone from the archdiocesan office. My mom told the lady she now realized the school would not be part of the Catholic school system. The lady said, "Whoever said it had to be Catholic? Couldn't you really serve more students if it were not a Catholic school?" During that phone call, my mom told her it would be developed as a Christian school. During the conversation, the lady from the archdiocese asked, "What will the school be named?" Together they listed the gifts of the Holy Spirit and when it came to the gift of wisdom, my mother said, "It will be named after the gift of wisdom." The lady from the archdiocese said, "That is Sophia."

My mom decided to hold two informational meetings in the fall of 1998. She used what she called her "kitchen money" to place a small ad in a parenting magazine. She designed the ad from clip art on Google, using a picture of a fingerprint with the tagline, "No Two Are Alike." This would become the logo for Sophia Academy. Looking back, the ad was pretty plain and un-compelling. Only a few people showed up for the first meeting, and the same thing happened at the second meeting. Although they thought it was a good idea, they did not sign on. My mom took two months off of this project and prayed, "God, if this school is going to happen, it is up to You."

At the third meeting, three families signed on to begin the school. When they left that night, my mom was excited but quickly realized what she had committed to. Now she really did have to start a school, and she had no idea how to do it.

Parents at the meeting asked, "Where is it going to be located?"

"I don't know," my mom replied.

"Who are the teachers going to be?"

"I don't have any teachers."

"What books and materials will you use?"

"I don't have any books and materials."

Sophia Academy, which had only been an idea, a hope and a dream, was now suddenly becoming a reality.

When my mom started working on how to promote the school, she realized there were a few stumbling blocks. She did not have a location, and most importantly, as my dad reminded her quite often, she did not have any students. The fact that three families had indicated interest in the school didn't mean they were coming. My mom was not prepared for someone to commit to the school, she didn't even have any contracts for them to sign. I remember my siblings and

I riding around in my mom's car every day searching for a location for the school. Whenever we stopped at a building, my mom told us to get out of the car and look around. We stopped at one building that was already a small private school. When we looked inside the building, it smelled horribly! The building was dark inside and looked as if it was not taken care of at all. As my mom took a look around, she asked us, "What do you all think? Do any of you like the building?" Without any hesitation, we all said, "No!"

However, God had everything arranged. After considering forty possible locations, a building was found. God sent my mom to the First Baptist Church located in Sandy Springs, which was a small congregation with a wonderful space for my mom to rent. This location would be able to offer three classrooms at a very reasonable rate. My sister Louise commented, "I remember going to the location of the school for the first few times, realizing that this was a new place that we would be going to a lot!"

God also sent my mom two teachers who were interested. God provided books and materials donated from other schools and purchased with tuition money. In order to begin a library in the school, my mom and some parents went to the Goodwill store and loaded up on the fifty-cent children's books. The cashier asked, "Why so many books?" When my mom told her what the books were for, the cashier made some of them a donation to the school. Goodwill Industries had given us our first taste of support from a community.

Sophia Academy started out with eleven students: me, two children from the same family, and eight other students whose parents were also looking for a Christian-based, specialized education program for their child. My mom acted as the founder and director of the school, as well as the development director, admissions director, business manager, carpool director, and chief janitor. My mom wanted the students to wear uniforms just as all of her other children wore uniforms to school.

It's hard to believe Sophia Academy was ever established. My brother Victor mentioned, "I was so young when it first started. I was five, not even in kindergarten when the school started. I do remember things were hectic. I knew that mom was trying to do something and that dad was helping her with it. The first thing I remember was that all the kids were really nice. My mom would always go through the halls and give around hugs to students. They would always say 'Mrs. Corrigan!' when she walked in. I thought my mom was famous and was always busy with the school."

My sister Mellie mentioned, "Mom worked really hard, and she was a really prayerful person. She did a good job of being a working mom, and she always helped me with whatever I needed."

My dad stated, "It was amazing to see my wife as the principal of the school, and she did a fantastic job! I saw some great results in my daughter, Caroline, who grew as a result of Sophia Academy. This school was a very nurturing atmosphere and environment and was all positive."

My mom not only wanted myself and other children to have the best education possible, but she also wanted a place for me and the other children to learn about faith and grow in it. She wanted the staff and faculty, including herself, to teach children and others who worked there, and everyone who walked into Sophia Academy, about God and faith, through Sophia Academy's mission. She wanted everyone to feel accepted about who they are in Christ, and to love themselves the way He loves us.

Carlton, a friend of my mom's, commented, "We *all* have learning differences. It's a blessing that the founder, Marie Corrigan, had the wisdom and insight to bring out each student's potential by nurturing these differences. This enables them to be productive members of society."

Anne, Director of Liturgy, stated, "From my own background in religious education, I know that faith-based schools play a unique and integral part in the education opportunity for students. All schools contribute heavily to the development of children's character and value systems. Faith-based schools nurture their students' souls along with their academic potential. Catholic schools especially prepare the whole person in mind, body, and spirit. In the world today, the moral compass is missing—we need Christian-based schools so that each lesson becomes multidimensional with faith, morals, and values infused into every part of that lesson, which in turn translates to our lives."

It was a sunny day. There was not a cloud in the sky, and school had been in session for months. One day, my mom left work early after she fired an employee. She was very frustrated at this situation, and she had been dealing with this young female teacher for months. This particular teacher did not want to follow the mission of the school or the dress code for teachers. One day, this young teacher came to school dressed in her boyfriend's baggy shirt and pants. My mom asked her about it, and she said, "I haven't had time to do any laundry." My mom gave her forty-five minutes to go to Target (which was five minutes away) to buy something appropriate and professional to wear.

My mom took control of this teacher's classroom, and after about an hour, the teacher returned in an appropriate shirt and a very tight skirt. When the teacher began teaching, the skirt split all the way to her waistline. The teacher immediately taped her skirt together, but the skirt split again, and she stapled it together. At this point, my mom was so frustrated! Between classes, my mom asked the teacher, "Do you really want to teach here?" And the teacher responded, "No!" My mom said, "That's perfect. Today is your last day, and you can leave immediately." The teacher did leave immediately, and my mom did not know what to do next. She asked the other teacher if she would bring all eleven students together, all varying ages, and watch over them for the rest of the day.

Afterward, my mom left school to drive home. As she was driving home, she was very upset, crying the whole way home. "Is this it, Lord? Is the school going to close? We've only been at this a few months," she said. As she drove into her garage, she noticed a man walking up the driveway. He was a painter she had employed once months before. The painter was dressed in a painter's suit, completely white without a spot of paint on it. She had talked to him some when he worked at our house, but the last thing she wanted to do in that moment when she arrived home was talk to this painter. He walked up to her door and said to her, "I've been thinking about you... .I wanted to give you this." He handed her a calendar with an eagle on the front, and then he turned and walked away. She opened the calendar, and inside was the scripture passage from Isaiah 40:29–31, "He giveth power to the faint, and to them that have no might he has given strength. Even the youth shall faint and be weary and the young men shall utterly fall, but they that wait upon the Lord shall renew their strength; they shall mount up with wings as eagles, they shall run and not be weary, and they shall walk and not be faint."

There was something my mom didn't know—the teacher who was fired immediately called the parents of all the students. She had many poor comments and judgment about the way the school was being run, the curriculum, and its possible future. Parents started calling my mom as soon as they heard from the former teacher. They wanted to meet with my mom right away, so a meeting was organized for that night. Somehow my mom felt strong, determined the school could weather this storm, but she was scared about what the possible fallout would be. My mom was very worried and concerned about the school, uncertain whether it would continue. She knew the only way was to trust God through all of this uncertainty. All the parents met together that evening, and when the meeting was over, they all were in support of Sophia Academy and my mom.

My mom depended so much on the remaining teacher, Amy, who was excellent. Amy remarked, "I thought I would just go straight into public school. I never, ever thought I would teach children with special needs. And I can remember being in college, and you had to choose a specialization. The smartest specialization to choose would have been to teach because there will always be that need, and it's always under-fulfilled. There are never enough teachers to teach special needs. It takes a special person, special needs, and I didn't think that was me. Fast forward to the future, and I took a job with Sophia Academy, which was literally being created day by day. I ended up loving it, and I was so invested in it. God definitely shaped me."

"I remember one student came from another big school, and for the first few days, if not weeks, he was in my classroom. He would sometimes stop what he was doing to sleep. He had learned in his last school just to disconnect from everything when he got frustrated. We taught in a multi-sensory way that captured all of the student's attention. See it, feel it, do it. No matter what the learning difference, there was a way for the student to receive the information and be able to have success. I also taught a child who was adopted, who had fetal alcohol syndrome and was not able to read at all. Even he experienced success, and more than that, he was accepted for the person that he was. You don't count on having a child with special needs. You don't count on having to send your kids to a special school. At first some of the parents were on the fence about what the school was going to be like. It's a brand-new school, and that's scary. And then they see their child happy and successful for the first time."

After another particularly hard day, my mom wondered again if the school would continue. She decided to drive to the mall. When she started driving, she said, "Lord, if You want the school to continue, *show me!*" When she arrived at the mall, almost immediately, she heard a mother call out to her child, "Sophia!" That was quick, but not enough to convince my mom. When she was finished shopping, she left the mall and started driving home. On the way home, she noticed a sign saying, "Sophia." That was odd, she thought. Just one word, but it could be a total coincidence. She made it home, and there was a package waiting on the front porch. Inside was a book entitled, *Christ Is My Life*, and the publisher was Sophia. My mom was standing in the foyer of our home, and she felt the most incredible force, a lifting up off of her feet, with Jesus telling her, "You will do this for me!" It was not a choice anymore, for now she understood that God did not mean for her to start this and stop it without Him telling her to.

Incredible growth began happening at the school, and within seven years, a nest egg for a future location of our own was big enough that we could make a move. Mom looked at many, many buildings trying to envision how they would be retrofitted for a school. She was looking for a property with some outdoor space for a playground as well as a possible gym in the future, plenty of parking and access from major highways. After a while, a location was found. Per our advancement director, Cathi, "There was obviously such a contrast between the church rental and the renovated building that was bought." The church was old and dingy, but there was enthusiasm from increased enrollment and the plans for a "home of our own." When we moved, we even painted a yellow brick road with families' names on it on the driveway, along with sayings like "There's no place like home." We were bursting with pride. Every child had a handprint tile, and these tiles lined all the hallways; this was a constant reminder of the school being "their school" and how much heart was in it.

## CHAPTER FOUR

# STUDENT AT SOPHIA ACADEMY

——

This would be a day I would not forget. Today was like no other. This day meant I would be attending a school that would change my life forever! It would be my first day spending time at a school that would hold a very special place in my heart. To me, this feeling would surpass any other feeling I had felt about anywhere else I had been. Yes, today would mark the start of a new beginning for me. I knew this place would meet all my expectations. All my questions, concerns, worries—I wouldn't have to search any further. I knew this was right where I was supposed to be! I had a feeling this day would be the best day ever—one of the best days of my life!

Today was my first day of attending school as a student at Sophia Academy!

I was super excited to wake up. I woke up right when my alarm started buzzing. I could hear my alarm clock buzzing as if it was right in my heart. I pushed the off button and got up. My heart was filled with joy and excitement. I had a big smile on my face. I was feeling very joyful and very ecstatic and ready for the day.

When walking down the stairs to the kitchen, I was surprised I didn't fall down from all the excitement. I literally felt like my heart would explode! I walked into the kitchen to eat breakfast. I saw my mom reading the newspaper and eating breakfast. My mom was quiet while I ate a doughnut—I know, healthy choice, right? She asked me how I felt about this day. I told her I was very excited about all that was planned. My dad was getting ready to leave for work as well. Before he left, he told my mom and I that he hoped today "is a great first day for us and that everything goes well." My sisters and brother were waiting for their carpool ride to arrive at our house. One of our neighbors would take my siblings to school since they all attended the same school at that time. I got my bookbag and lunchbox ready and walked to the door into the garage. When I got in my mom's car, I chose to sit in the front seat as I wanted to sit next to her. My mom always listened to Christian music in the car. She asked if I wanted to listen to Twila Paris on the way to school. I had grown up listening to Twila and loved her songs, so I said, "Yes!" We listened to every song on the CD until we arrived at school. As my mom was driving us, I could feel such peace and joy in my heart. One of Twila's songs on the CD was called "God Is In Control." We were both listening and singing to the song. I could see my mom was excited for the day too. She looked very focused and ready to conquer the day.

When we arrived at school, my mom decided to drive in behind the school. My mom then took a breath, looked at me, and said she wanted to keep listening to Twila Paris and pray before she went into the building. She prayed to God, telling Him she wanted everyone at the school to have a great first day. Then we got out of her car and walked to the front entrance of the school. The building already had lights on inside because there were teachers setting up their rooms, waiting for students to come in their classrooms.

My mom and I then went into her office, which looked neat and organized and felt formal and precise. The walls were white, and a desk was in the middle of the room. There were filing cabinets on either side of the room against the walls, and there was a bookcase against the wall in front of the desk. There were two chairs on either side of the door when you first walked into her office. My mom wanted to get everything ready and organized before the school day started. I decided to walk into my homeroom classroom to put my bookbag into my specific cubby so I wouldn't forget about putting it away later.

My mom thought it would make more sense since it was the first day of school for the students to have a half day. She didn't want the students to feel overwhelmed and overloaded with too much information right away. She thought it would be better for us to be familiar with everything before we started a long day of school. Much to my excitement, I decided to start introducing myself to people. I had the biggest smile on my face and felt confident about telling them who I was. The students I met were nice and friendly, and I noticed two of them were from the school I attended the year before Sophia Academy.

When the bell rang, it was time for all the students to go to their own classrooms for homeroom. We took our seats at our desks, and our teacher stood up from her desk and walked toward the front of the room to introduce herself. There was a schedule written on the board of what every day would look like, followed by times to be in specific locations in the school.

After homeroom, we got in a line and met in the hallway. My mom wanted everyone to meet in the gym because she wanted to give us a tour of the school and have us become familiar with everything. The tour was only forty-five minutes long, during which she showed us all the rooms in the building. When the tour was over, she told us she wanted our photo to be taken for our first day of school. We all went outside across the front of the building for our photo shoot. Since it was summer, it was still hot outside; I could feel the humidity as soon as the sun touched my face. When the photo was finished, we all went back inside to have our first class of the day.

The first class I had was math, and back then—as well as even now—math was not my strong suit. Five students were in my math class. In the big classroom, there was a green chalkboard against the wall, and there were desks lined up with chairs for students. Our teacher had a very upbeat and energetic personality. She was really good at teaching this math class and for the first time I understood concepts that I had never understood before. It was amazing!

The next and last class I had for the day was English, which I absolutely loved. I had a different teacher for this class and really enjoyed having this woman as a teacher. She also had an energetic and upbeat personality. I had always enjoyed English and writing, but I could tell I was going to enjoy it even more now. This lady really knew how to engage us in the content and get us to meet the challenges of the coursework.

When class was over, the first day of Sophia Academy was over. At noon, our homeroom teachers directed us to the area where carpool would be. We all stood and waited for our parents to pick us up. When the students left, it was just the teachers, as well as my mom and I. My mom spent a few minutes speaking with the teachers about how their first day was. When she was finished, I followed her to her office so we could get our things ready to leave to go home. When she was ready, we walked to her car to leave to drive home.

From that day onward, being a student at Sophia Academy was amazing! Attending this school for the four years I did filled me with so much joy. These were the best years of my life as a student. If I had the chance to relive these days again, there would be no doubt in my mind I would. Attending a school such as Sophia Academy taught me so much about myself as well as the love of God. It taught me how to love myself and others the way Christ loves us. It taught me how to depend on God alone for everything I needed and wanted, that He would always provide for my needs. Most importantly, though, this school taught me who God is as a person. This school showed me how to have a relationship with Him.

Many memories flood my mind when I think of my days as a student at Sophia Academy. Memories such as when the teachers took the students to Key West for a week-long trip to learn about the ocean and sea, the Love Letter Production that incorporated the story of my mom starting a school, field days at the school on the last day before summer started, becoming an ambassador at the school, Christmas concerts we performed for our parents and families, and so much more! These are the memories that will stay in my heart forever.

When I was a student at Sophia Academy, God taught me every day how to have confidence in myself, to believe in myself, and to have joy. I could see him working through my mother, through the teachers, through and for the students.

We all were progressing, and the school was growing quickly. He was all around the school, in every person, in every situation, even when you did not expect Him.

What I loved most about being a student at Sophia Academy was seeing it all from the very beginning. Sophia Academy was a baby when I first saw it, and I watched it grow throughout the years. Watching this school grow from the ground up made me so much more grateful for this place. Realizing I took part in this journey with so many other people made these years much more extraordinary.

Sophia Academy was always on my mom's mind, day and night, weekends and holidays. My family and I would often say the school was an additional child of hers, which it was in a way. For as much time as she spent on the school, it was all worth it. She did everything in her power to make Sophia Academy the best place it could be. I, for one, definitely know she made God proud, and I am so proud of her for making this school for me and for other students with learning differences.

## CHAPTER FIVE

# LIFE AFTER SOPHIA ACADEMY

———

It was the end of my eighth-grade year, and summer was approaching. Sophia Academy did not yet have a high school when I finished that year. Without having a high school in place, I appealed to my mom continuously to get one started. What I didn't understand at the time was how expensive it was to start a high school. As much as she would have wanted for the students to continue through twelfth grade, it would take a lot of funding, more than we had anticipated.

I wanted to freeze time and never leave.

Unbeknownst to me, God was telling me to trust Him; He had me in the palm of His hand. Even in a new school, He would still be with me every step of the way. He was telling me, "You do not understand now, but there is a reason this happened. I will be with you and I will never leave you." My parents determined which high school I should go to. Coming from a school I had loved so much, this was the last thing I wanted to do. I was frightened and unsure of the future, and I was not ready to leave this place. I would have to say goodbye for now.

The day I left Sophia Academy, negative thoughts were coming into my head telling me I would never be this comfortable again. Even worse, these thoughts told me God left me when I left Sophia Academy, but I didn't realize this until I began attending high school.

When I started high school, I felt different from the way I did at Sophia Academy. Joy, calmness, and no fear of being myself—these feelings were now gone. I felt the complete opposite. I did not know who I was anymore. God did not forget about me, though; He was in disguise in my teachers and people I met at my high school.

I did not have a lot of friends at this school—close to none would be the most fitting answer. People bullied me due to my petite size and shyness. During PE, I wouldn't be picked for any of the teams. The coach would assign me to one, but it was obvious the team didn't want me. There were many more boys at the school, but even the small group of girls excluded me. I learned to deal with the lack of female friendships, though, because their conversations were often about things that frightened me like drugs, alcohol, and personal relationships with some of the male students. I wasn't uninformed about sex, drugs, and alcohol—my parents had talked to us about those things from the time we were very young. But I wasn't interested in these things. I just wanted to do my best in school and reach the goals I had set for myself.

The enemy would whisper to me each day when I walked through the halls, in class, and when I was alone, telling me, "Caroline, you're too shy. No one will like you if you're this way. No one will accept you for the true person you are. Talk more and be more like the students of this school. If you act the way these students are acting, people will like you more and accept you more. God put you in this situation at this school because He does not love you. He wants nothing to do with you." All throughout the day, I heard various lies from the enemy. More than ever, the feelings of insecurity, anxiety, and self-doubt crept in. These fears, these thoughts, these feelings that were in the pit of my heart and soul, were surfacing where everyone could see them, even when I didn't want them to.

One day, a teacher had us complete a grammar assignment. I worked on it all night until the early hours of the next morning. When I received a grade back from my teacher, I was shocked to find it was an F. Confused at why this happened, and getting no explanation from the teacher, I asked her why she gave me this grade. She looked at me, and with a strong and blunt tone, said, "Well, Caroline, you deserved it! You did not work hard on this assignment at all!" When I heard this, I couldn't believe it. I asked her if I could do anything to make up this grade, but she became very frustrated and bitter toward me. This wasn't the first time this particular teacher had treated me in this manner. It's humiliating to be talked to like this. All I needed were more details about how to complete the assignment correctly. We could have easily come to a solution, but she gave me no time for a discussion. I came to understand through years of experience that many teachers want to work with students who have learning differences, and therefore work with smaller groups of students, but these teachers don't have the personality and perseverance, much less the training sometimes, to deal with students who need much more support. This teacher had no tolerance for students with learning differences. The administration came to realize this, and the teacher was dismissed shortly after this incident.

I can't see the future—no one can. But how could a person such as God who loves His child so much put her in a situation like this? Why did He want this to happen? He was teaching me that, when I left Sophia Academy, these things were happening for a reason. Many times, I felt very ashamed of the person I was. I felt as if He was punishing me. Many days, I felt alone, as if no one cared for me or wanted anything to do with me. I felt very distant from God. Each time I felt like this, in the depths of my heart, God would tell me He has me in the palm of His hand and is watching over me. "Do not worry, my child. I am with you always and will never leave you." He told me there were multiple reasons He put me through this situation. God knew I would be able to handle it, and He is a God of LOVE. In Him, I am strong. In Him, I can do all things through Christ who strengthens me. He was also preparing me for challenges to come.

On another day, while waiting to be picked up after school, I asked the after-school director a question. I could tell she was annoyed by the way she responded—extremely curt and derogatory. While waiting for a tour to start, one parent in the group saw me and started a conversation with me, asking what my name was. Before I could respond, the after-school director looked at me, then looked at the parent and said, "Don't worry about her! She's not important!" Again, the after-school director was about to take part in a tour—I acknowledge she was busy. It takes a special kind of teacher to teach students who have special learning needs, but the administration also needs to be trained about specific learning needs. Any person who interacts with a student with learning differences needs to understand that directions need to be clear and concise, and the student needs the opportunity to ask questions. That's all I wanted, such a simple thing. It makes all the difference in the success or failure of a student's day at school.

Eventually, I survived high school and graduated. My family was very excited about me graduating high school, and I was very excited about it as well! To be honest, because of my learning difference, I did not think or believe I would make it this far and graduate high school. God's plans are way bigger than what I had thought and dreamed of.

When it was a few months before my graduation, I surprised myself with an accomplishment I didn't know I was capable of. The principal at our school had talked to us about giving a high school speech at graduation. When I came home after hearing this, I told my mom about it and asked her if she thought it would be a good idea. She automatically said "Yes!" I was nervous because I had never given a speech before, let alone stand before people I did not know and speak to them. Because of my usually-timid personality, this made me very nervous and self-conscious. My mom was very sweet and offered her help and time. I rehearsed the speech multiple times, including how I would walk up to the podium, adjust the microphone, take a deep breath, and launch into the words I wanted to share with the audience.

The principal offered practice rehearsal days to those of us who were giving speeches, and I went to every single one to make sure I felt ready for this day. The closer graduation came, the more confident I felt. Over a thousand people were attending the graduation. I remember my family sitting as close as they could, watching me, taking photos of me, smiling at me, and so happy for me to reach this milestone in my life. When it was time for me to walk up to the podium to start my speech, I felt as if my body was about to explode—I was full of excitement and so much energy! By committing to this speech, I realized I can do all things through Christ who strengthens me. God was showing me and teaching me in that moment that I am capable of anything and everything because of who I am in Him.

At the end of the speech, I got a standing ovation! I was giggling inside because I thought people would never stop clapping. When graduation ended and my classmates and I walked down the aisle after receiving our diplomas, I smiled so much that my cheeks hurt. When I walked into the auditorium with the other graduates, not only did my family greet me with hugs, so many strangers approached me and told me my speech was the best high school speech they had ever heard! I was so proud of myself. I felt on top of the world. This was one of the best moments of my life!

In 2007, I started attending college. My college years definitely taught me some life lessons as well. My roommates were three other girls who I had absolutely nothing in common with. I had gone through the school admission office in order to find roommates, and this is how things worked out. Typically, I kept to myself and I would go home most weekends. I did join a sorority that offered me a lot of activities and opportunities to be with other wonderful young women. I especially liked the service projects; the joy of service to others has followed me throughout my adult life.

My college adviser, Mike Chambers, was very helpful to me. He was the director of the Student Disability Resource Center, and he was the one who introduced me to assistive technology. Assistive technology is any device to assist students with learning differences to achieve maximum success. Mr. Chambers is one of the kindest and most professional administrators I have ever met. He worked so hard to pair students with specific teachers who understood different learning styles as well as provide us tools such as laptops, iPads, and headphones to assist us with our assignments. Whenever I needed direction or clarification, he would be there to help. Every time I think of Mr. Chambers, I ask God to send him a special blessing for all the people he has helped.

I graduated in 2011 with a degree in general studies, cum laude with a 3.6 GPA. I had accomplished so much. I had exceeded my expectations, and I knew I was on to greater things.

CHAPTER SIX

# EMPLOYED AT SOPHIA ACADEMY

———

After graduating college, I was honored and flattered to take a position at Sophia Academy. It was a few days after graduating college that my mom asked me if I wanted to work at the school. After seeing how assistive technology had helped me so much, she wanted to develop this as part of the Sophia Academy curriculum. My response was, "Yes, of course!"

The only position available was to work part-time with the preschool director. There were four to five children in the preschool, and each one of them needed specialized attention. I talked over a plan with the director, and she selected two students to receive assistive technology support. The students really enjoyed the devices and the programs, and they immediately showed improvement. We were on a roll! We knew there were so many other students in the school who could also benefit.

Initially, my mom hired a teacher who had some experience with assistive technology. I was to be her assistant, and I handled all of the lower school students. I worked with them frequently throughout the week, and I wrote weekly reports for their parents. My mom had a parent make a sign that said

"Assistive Technology" that was placed at an entrance door at the end of the school building. We also served students after school who came from other schools. They too made progress using assistive technology. Later, our assistive technology director would take a position at another school and I would become the director.

Sophia Academy was always a relatively small school. What started with eleven students ballooned to over 175 students within a matter of a few years. But, as with all specialized schools, they are expensive, and parents are always eager to move their child to a nonspecialized school where there is little or no stigma about their learning style. For this reason, the number of students per year was always questionable. Many parents spent their spring and summer searching for other, less-expensive, regular-education schools for their child. When this didn't work out, because their child still needed specialized instruction, they would return for admission. They were always welcomed to return, and it was exciting to see new students join the school each year.

During the summers working at Sophia Academy, I worked with the Leadership Institute, which was also developed by my mom. Each Leadership Institute had a theme, and she would create a week-long curriculum including many field trips. Hospitals, jails, businesses, museums, historic landmarks, and historic restaurants were always part of the curriculum. I will never forget visiting the Dekalb County Jail for juveniles. Each one of us had to be screened before entering the jail. It was so sad and disturbing to see so many youths behind bars. We then went into the courtroom to witness the process of juveniles being released or held further for their crimes. Many of the juveniles did not have parents present to support them but perhaps had an aunt, uncle, or cousin promising the youth would do a better job if given the chance. Sadly, we did not see many of the young prisoners released.

Anne, who was the Director of Liturgy, remarked, "The 2015 Christmas program was a special script written by my husband and daughter. They retold the story of the birth of Jesus with the special help of a writer by the name of Saint Luke, played by one of our high school students. As Saint Luke wrote his Gospel, three different angels came to advise the fictional Saint Luke and help him see the real meaning behind Jesus's birth. Every student in the school had a role and appeared on stage dressed in costume. The students worked to learn lines, handle props, manage entrances and exits, and gain a little understanding into what goes on in staging a theatrical production."

"The following year, the students presented a totally different Christmas program. This time, the story of Jesus's birth was told through the eyes of the three wise men—using puppets. Again, a role was found for each student—every one of whom who had a puppet—dressed in costume. As you can imagine, several students didn't want to participate. Many of our students struggled with anxiety issues, which can present themselves through physical and emotional symptoms. They often can have difficulty functioning in a stressful situation such as a public performance. But in the end, every student was involved and came through brilliantly. The use of puppets was a great anxiety self-help. By using puppets, and having something to focus on other than themselves, the students became great performers, and each contributed to the overall success in telling the Christmas story. The students were not as self-conscious about themselves because everyone was 'playing a part.' It was the puppet that was the center of attention."

"Two particular students come to mind. I won't mention them here by name, but their names will forever be written on my heart and mind. One student was very shy and suffered from severe anxiety when put in a social situation. He really didn't want to participate, or dress up, or have a puppet. But once he saw the others doing those things—and having a great time—he tried it too. That evening, after the program was over, he excitedly came up to me and said, 'When are we going to do another program?' What a thrill! And, as a postscript, he went on to high school, where he participated in their theater ministry. That was definitely God winking at us!"

"Another student was also very shy and only communicated in a whisper. She too was very hesitant to participate in the program, but quickly got involved when she was assigned with helping with the movements of a large, almost life-size puppet. It required her to move the puppet's mouth and arms during the program. She took on the task, and after weeks of program preparation and rehearsals, she was communicating loud and clear with the stage manager and me. She even asked questions to clarify her staging, movements, etc. Another wink from God!"

There was a yearly summer project that my siblings and I hated…moving the library. Because the school was growing at such a rapid rate, we had to keep adding to the library to meet state standards for media resources. This meant going out and getting more books and taking donations from other schools. Additional shelves had to be purchased and set up. My mom would hire students from other schools to come and help us, it was such a big job! Day-in and day-out, for usually a week, we hauled the books from one place to another. We then had to go back to the empty classroom where the books had been and set it up for students. This meant more desks and chairs were needed. My mom would make another trip to a warehouse in South Atlanta and buy the furniture that was needed from a surplus store. Our next project? Clean the new furniture. This summer job taught me hard work and responsibility.

My mom had a fabulous assistant, Melissa. Melissa has fond memories of the school and has said, "God was always around, challenging us to challenge ourselves and the school. Summer reading and learning was not just for the kids, but for faculty and staff. We were always challenged to take in more information on how children learn and how to incorporate God into their learning so they have faith and meaning. Something to fall back on in addition to what they were learning in school."

We were always looking for ways to inform the greater community and promote the school. One summer, my mom had the great idea to have me and my two sisters deliver cakes to all of the newspaper and parent magazine writers that had written about the school or we hoped would write about the school. These were the years before GPS. Each of us left the school with our cars packed full of cakes and a list of addresses for delivery. The day was sweltering hot. It was a terrible assignment, and each of us called the school repeatedly to ask for directions from my mom. When the day was done, the cakes were delivered, but my sisters and I swore we would never take on that assignment again.

The idea of adding a high school was always on the agenda. But how to do it? It was going to take a lot more funding, and we needed ways to encourage students to want to be at Sophia

Academy. One thing we lacked was a gym. My mom and our advancement director, Cathi, devised a plan to raise the money for the project. A contractor was selected, and we had to make the decision to start immediately because the price of steel was set to be raised. Without all the money in hand, but with a heart full of faith, the project was started. The fundraising went well, but simultaneously, my mom was getting sick. She was diagnosed with a rare cancer and treatment began. For two years, she was treated unsuccessfully, and it was determined that a stem cell transplant would be needed.

For now, gone were the days when she could quickly walk around the entire campus. Her walking was slow and labor intensive and very painful. She was admitted to the hospital on January 11, had almost every complication possible, and could not come home until forty-five days later. She was so weak that she didn't know when she would be able to return to the school, but she wanted to come back and looked forward to the day that would happen. Cathi had become a dear friend of my mom's and someone my mom could really count on. While my mom was in the hospital and then recuperating, Cathi was in charge. It was a really tough time, and Cathi remembers, "Many ways of His presence came to Marie through signs and people who showed up at the times she needed it most to keep her stamina and also answering prayers. I really learned that many times you have tried everyone and are losing hope when God provides the answer. For me, it taught me that you seem to see his Glory more when you have tried much and are weak on your knees when He appears." My mom eventually returned as director.

***

During my time as an employee, I started dating my now-husband, Chris. One day, Chris and I decided to take a day trip to the place where I attended college. I was very excited about showing him all around where I went to school since he had never seen the campus before. Since it was cold at that time of year, we wore long sleeved shirts, long pants, and tennis shoes. The trip took over two hours to drive from where we were living at the time, but we were both very excited about this day trip together.

When we arrived in Milledgeville, memories started rushing into my mind from all the experiences I had in school. It was very cold, but this, surprisingly, did not bother me as much because of the way I was feeling about this day. When we got out of our car, I decided to show him where I would often go to eat meals. I then showed him some of the buildings where I took classes. Since it was a weekend, we did not see many people there.

The next building I was about to show Chris was the one I had been preparing myself for, the Student Disability Resource Center. I had not yet told him I had a learning difference, and I was very frantic and paralyzed in my mind, worrying about his reaction. I was even contemplating whether or not I should tell him. Before meeting Chris, I did not have to tell people I had a learning disability because people already knew that I did. The reason I was very nervous about telling him was because I thought of the worst-case scenario: he would judge me and think less of me. Even worse, he would leave me for telling him. I was very private about this information and didn't like people knowing this about me for these reasons. When we walked to the building, I was excited but nervous. I tried hard not to show this, but on the inside, I was shaking uncontrollably at the thoughts running through my mind.

"What if I tell him and he thinks less of me?"

"What if I tell him and he won't know what to think or how to respond?"

"Should I just not tell him, and we leave to drive home?"

On the drive down to Milledgeville, I decided in my mind I would tell Chris. Yes, I was nervous about his reaction, but—at the same time—what was the worst that could happen, despite what my thoughts were telling me? I decided to give in and tell him. When we walked to this building, I looked at him and said, "I wanted to show you this building because this is where I spent a lot of time." He was so kind and thoughtful with his response. I could tell he was very confused. He said in reply, "This is very nice that you are showing me this building, but why?" I decided to ignore what my body was doing in this moment and said, "I have something to tell you. I have a learning difference." When I finished telling him, he just gave me the biggest smile and said, "Caroline, you are so brave to tell me this. I love you so much more—not because you have this, but because you told me. That was very brave of you!" I was shocked with his response! No one I knew had ever told me that before. I was very relieved with what he said. Finally, someone who accepts me for me and not for what I have, I thought. After I heard his response, I was so completely overwhelmed with joy and relief that I gave him a big hug!

This is one of the many ways God shows His love to us. Yes, we all have differences, and yes, we all have flaws. God does not want us to hide them from Him. He wants us to come as we are to Him, broken, to put us back together, and He accepts us with everything we have because we are His children. We are His sons and daughters in Christ. He loves us too much not to turn away, and He loves us despite what we do not like about ourselves. He loves us more than we can imagine.

## CHAPTER SEVEN

# GOD IS SOPHIA ACADEMY

---

What do I think about God and Sophia Academy? Well, a lot of things—they are very similar to each other. The moment I stepped through the doors of Sophia Academy, I knew I had found the school. This school had everything I wanted and needed. This school I had been waiting so long for was worth the wait. When I look back and think about the previous experiences I had in school, everything God put me through was worth it. Every experience was a setup for success. All the negative feelings I used to have went away when I stepped inside the building of Sophia Academy. Everything I had been looking for, searching for, hoping for, and dreaming of, finally came to fruition.

Everything I wanted and needed in a school was an answered prayer from God. This strengthened my relationship with Him in an amazing and profound way. God gave me exactly what I wanted in a school, even the things I didn't even think of praying for. God knew my desires as much as He knew my parents' and other families' desires. So many parents had clearly been praying for a better school for their children. They too wanted a rigorous curriculum, extracurriculars, and a safe and secure environment.

God says that the bigger the burden, the bigger the blessing. It is so true! Not only did I experience burdens, but
my parents did as well. When Sophia Academy came alive,
this dream God put in my mom's heart to start this school—
although a lot of work—changed not just my life but many
people's lives. Our entire family was involved with the school
on some level. Sophia Academy was the answer many people
were looking for.

When I think about Sophia Academy, yes, the first word
that comes to mind is "school." "Community," "acceptance,"
"worth," and "faith" are just a few of many words to describe
this school. There are many joyful memories of that amazing place.

When I was a student and an employee at Sophia Academy, toward the end of the day, it was so nice to have chapel,
which turned into Mass when Sophia became a Catholic
school. It was reassuring and extremely relaxing to focus on
the presence of God and nothing but Him in that hour. Being
in the presence of God is so beautiful. It is so captivating as
well to worry about nothing, just focusing on your time with
Him. It was also amazing to see all the students that attended
Sophia when I was there as an employee. Seeing them as
students took me back to when I was a student.

Even though God wanted my mom to start a school for
me and children with learning differences, I believe He also
wanted Sophia Academy to be created as a place for people to
learn and know about Him as well. This is also what my mom
wanted for the school. When I think of Sophia Academy as
a place of love, acceptance, gentleness, and kindness, that is
who God is. God is a person who loves His children dearly
and so much more than we can imagine! God goes above and
beyond each day to show His love for us, and He accepts each

of His children for who they are. God is merciful, forgiving, encouraging, wonderful, amazing, full of hope and healing, and much more. God worked through my mom each and every day to do anything to make each child happy. This is how God is—He will do anything he can just to put a smile on our faces. He wants us to be happy, more than happy—He wants us to be joyful in Him.

When I am in the presence of God, I can tell him anything and all things that are on my heart because I know He will listen. When we stand before God in His presence, we can be ourselves. God made us perfectly imperfect to perform a work in us. In the world, we are imperfect, but to Him, we are perfect in His eyes. God loves each and every one of us the same amount. No one is less or more than the other; we all have the same worth and value. Even though each of us at Sophia had a learning disability, we were accepted and loved. God accepts us even with our flaws or weaknesses. Even what we don't like, God loves that. As the Sophia Academy faculty and staff were encouraging and supporting of one another, so God is with us. Yes, God will support you with whatever you do in your life. He will meet you right where you are.

At Sophia Academy, I was different from others—I felt and acted the way God wanted me to be, feeling joyful and being myself. I stopped listening to the world and, most importantly, stopped focusing on who the world wanted me to be. By taking my eyes off of the world, I put my eyes on God.

The reason I wrote this chapter is to tell you, my friend, that you are not who the world says you are. We are who God says we are. God says:

- You are a masterpiece.
- You are beautifully and wonderfully made.

- You are strong.
- You are capable.
- You are the daughter/son of the King.
- You are the apple of His eye.

There are so many positive and wonderful and amazing words that God says you are. God loves you so much!

God wants nothing more but for you to have a relationship with Him. He is always watching over you, protecting you, and showing you His love. God is a person. God has feelings. He wants you to have a relationship with Him. He wants to be your best friend. He wants you to love him. He will never force His love on you. He is not that sort of person and will never be.

I am relating Sophia Academy to God's love. When stepping through the doors of Sophia Academy, I experienced nothing but peace and calm. While I was at Sophia Academy, both as a student and an employee, I believed I could be the person I was meant to be. I was never afraid of being myself at Sophia Academy. I knew no matter how I acted, or what I said, or didn't say, that God would still remain the same and love me. This is what God wants for us. He wants us to be the person we are meant to be, the person He made us to be. He wants us to live our true potential—which is how he sees us. He wants this for you because of how much He loves you and always will. God is nothing but good. God is LOVE. Yes, He is LOVE. That is such an important word. When you think of LOVE, this is what God is. He will always love you no matter what. He will always stay the same. He does not have an end and no beginning. He will never leave you.

God loves us so much that He does not want to leave us where we are. He wants to move us for growth and change so He can see us grow for bigger and better things because He knows we have more potential in us. He will never stop loving us even if we stop loving Him. God is our Father in Heaven. He wants nothing but good things for us, for He is a Father who is faithful, good, and merciful. His love endures forever, and He will never stop loving us for as long as we are on this earth.

## CHAPTER EIGHT

# WHAT MADE SOPHIA
# ACADEMY DIFFERENT

---

My mom really wanted the school to be based in the Catholic faith, and she was interested in speaking to archbishop about making this happen. She believed deep in her heart that this is what God wanted for the school. Sophia Academy started out as a Christian school. My mom wanted people to learn about the Catholic faith.

My mom told me a few days prior to this day we would be driving to the Archdiocese of Atlanta, located in Smyrna, to speak with the archbishop to make Sophia a Catholic faith-based school. I had known for a long time that this was very important to my mom because our family is Catholic, and she thought it would be in the best interest of the school.

It was the fall of 2011. I woke up early that morning to get ready for the day and knew that it would be a great day! From the moment I woke up, I felt very relaxed and clear of thought. It was as if God had removed what was on my mind the previous night to when I woke up this specific morning; I only focused on Him and Him alone. It was a clear fall day without a single cloud in the sky. I wore a long, brown dress that had flowers stitched on it stopping at my knee, along with brown pantyhose with brown boots to match.

Since the meeting was supposed to start at 8:30 a.m., we arrived at 7:50 a.m. to make sure everyone who needed to be at this meeting was present. When we arrived at the Archdiocese, my mom's face looked hopeful but nervous at the same time. She then took my hand, and we began praying, "Hail Mary, full of grace, the Lord is with thee…" We also prayed an "Our Father, who art in heaven…" When we were finished saying these prayers, I looked up at her and said, "Mom, everything will be great! God has a plan!"

My mom and I both got out of the car and began walking together toward the building. When we walked inside, I was still feeling hopeful, but I was nervous about meeting the archbishop. However, I was also looking forward to the meeting and knew I had nothing to worry about. Besides, I did not have to participate in any of the discussion. The only reason I attended this meeting was to represent myself for the school, and also because my mom wanted me to be at the meeting to support her and the rest of the Sophia Academy staff and faculty.

When we all sat down in our seats, the archbishop began talking to us about why we were here. My mom stood up and told him she wanted Sophia Academy to become a Catholic faith-based school. She also mentioned the fact that, since it was God's plan and will for her to create this school, she believed He would want the school to be Catholic in order for the students to learn about the Catholic faith. The archbishop listened very intently to what she was saying. As I was looking at him and paying attention to what he was saying as well, I could see he believed this was very important to my mom, for myself, and for everyone who worked and was a student at Sophia Academy.

As my mom was saying these words, tears started running down her face very quickly, as if she couldn't stop herself from crying. While she was crying, she said, "This would mean a lot to me, and everyone at Sophia Academy, for this school to become a Catholic-faith-based school. Please consider this decision." As each person in the room listened to what she said, the archbishop stood up and said, "This school means a lot to you, doesn't it?"

My mom said, "Yes, it would mean the world to me for this to happen. This would mean a lot to my daughter, Caroline, and for everyone at Sophia Academy." The more my mom spoke, the faster her tears were streaming down her face. They were streaming so fast that she couldn't stop them from falling. Her face was red and blotchy from using a tissue to wipe the tears from her face.

Each person was studying every word she was saying, staying very focused, and listening as if she were the only person in the room. Her body was quivering from the words she was saying. She knew this would be an end-all situation, no matter what happened. Even though I did not tell her at the time, when people listened to what she said about how important this was to her, I thought, "They have to consider this. They have to. What else does she have to do to get their attention? Sophia Academy will become a Catholic school!" When my mom was finished speaking, the archbishop told her he and the rest of his team would come together to think about a decision on what to do, and they would let her know in a few days.

When the meeting was finished, we stood up from our seats and began leaving to walk out the door toward our cars.

As we got up from our seats, one by one, people walked over to my mom and gave her a hug, telling her she did a very good job with what she said. When my mom and I got back inside her car, she looked at me and said, "Caroline, I really hope this works!"

"I know it will!" I replied, and we drove home.

On our way home, I was still very calm as I had been since I woke up that morning. My mom was feeling calm as well, while at the same time anxiously awaiting to hear what the answer would be. We were both silent on the drive home. My mom was praying silently in her head, hoping the people she spoke to would consider this decision and approve it.

When we arrived home, my dad and siblings were waiting to hear how the meeting went. We told them the meeting went well and we hoped the archbishop will consider this decision. A few days later, my mom received a call telling her they decided to have Sophia Academy approved to be a Catholic-faith-based school.

When my mom received the call confirming the decision, she told us the big news. When she told us what she had heard, she looked very overjoyed and relieved that she had finally heard an answer. We were overjoyed at this news, and we couldn't stop praising God for this happening!

This story is about the day when the 9/11 attack occurred on September 11, 2001. Since I was unaware about what happened, I thought of the day just like any ordinary day at school. I remember sitting at my desk while the other students in the classroom with me were working on classwork. Out of nowhere, we all heard my mom over the intercom say, "Hello, I need everyone's attention. I need everyone to report to the chapel at this time. Thank you." I remember looking at my friends, along with the rest of the students and my teacher, wondering what had happened.

As I looked at the students' faces, everyone looked very confused but intrigued to know why we needed to be in the chapel. None of the other students knew why we needed to report there. I believe the teachers knew; however, they did not want to alarm us or scare us in any way. Our teacher told us to be very quiet while walking in the hallway to the chapel. Since the chapel was upstairs, we had to walk through the hallway and then up two flights of stairs. While walking into the hallway with the other students, I remember seeing that the lights were dimmed. The walls were filled with artwork from me and the other students from the school. The hallway by the staircase had a gray floor with white walls, and a black staircase led up to the rest of the classrooms and the chapel. I remember seeing yellow chairs formed in lines, and I do not remember hearing any noise when entering the room.

When we entered the room, the rest of the students along with their teachers followed behind us to sit down. When everyone was in the chapel, my mom waited for a few minutes for everyone to be seated. Once people were seated, my mom stood up, walked up to the front of the chapel and said, "I have brought you all here today to tell you that there has been a tragedy that has happened in our country today." I remember my mom, when she was telling us this information, trying her best to keep her composure while at the same time trying not to sob tears of sadness because of what she had told us. Her face looked very sad and hurt at the news she had informed us with. Before she gave us details, she wanted us to be quiet, and I remember looking at her, wanting to know more about this tragedy.

Even though I was a young child and did not fully understand what it all meant, I could feel pain and sadness in my heart. As I began looking around the room, faculty members and staff began crying, while at the same time trying to keep their composure. After my mom told us the news, she asked if we had any questions. When I looked around at each person's face, everybody was very quiet and yet in shock. The students did not know what to say, and neither did I. I do not remember what the students asked, if they asked any questions at all. At one point, I asked my mom if she could walk over to where I was, because I wanted to ask her a specific question. I was sitting down at this point, and she sat down next to me in another chair.

I was interested to know if anything had happened to one of my favorite stores in New York, a popular toy shop called FAO Schwarz. I looked at my mom, who was sitting next to me, and I whispered in her ear, "Mom, is FAO Schwarz okay?"

She looked back at me, giving me a reassuring smile followed by a giggle, and then replied with, "Yes, FAO Schwarz is okay. That is a very sweet question for you to ask." After we asked questions we had regarding the attack, my mom wanted us to sit in silence and pray for everyone who had passed, along with their families and everyone living in New York. My mom then proceeded to lead us in prayer with our chairs sitting in a circle. When the prayer ended, my mom told everyone to return back to class and resume their regular day. Everyone stood up, and one by one, we all followed each other back to our rooms.

My mom enjoyed seeing people receive awards for their good work in what they did at school. Given that Sophia Academy was a faith-based school, she had the idea of giving a person a character trait award, whether they were a student, staff member, or faculty member. She liked the idea of everyone being recognized for a virtue each month because she knew everyone mattered at the school. Once a month, these awards were given to people who demonstrated a virtue from the Bible. Each month, there would be a sheet that had the name of the month. The sheet mentioned the name of the person receiving this award, along with the reason why. For example, if a Character Trait was honor for that month, my mom would write on the sheet why this specific person would be receiving that award. The day it came time to have this award presented, the winner would have the award given to them. When this person received this award, they would be given the opportunity to pick two students they believed showed the same virtue. The three people would then have their photo taken. This award procedure was shown to exemplify what type of school Sophia Academy was and what this meant.

It was the month of April, and the Character Trait Award of the month was Courageous. Just like every month, a sheet for the awards was placed in everyone's mailbox located in the front reception office. When I received this sheet, I had put the name of the person I thought would best be suited for this award, as well as the reason why. Only the faculty and staff voted for the person of the month to have a certain Character Trait Award. When I finished filling out the sheet, I put it face-down back in my mailbox because I did not want anyone to see who I had chosen. Little did I know though, I was the person who would be receiving this award.

Toward the end of Mass, the award would be presented. Every Monday, we would have Mass in the afternoons. The chapel where Mass was performed was located near the cafeteria, and the Mass was always so beautifully performed. You could really feel the presence of God each time you stepped in the room.

When walking in the room and looking straight ahead, there was an altar and a cloth to lay the Roman hymnal when it was time for communion during Mass. There was an altar server cross in front of the altar, and directly below on the floor were kneelers for altar servers to kneel on. When walking in from the other side of the room, there was a piano that Anne, Director of Liturgy, would sit at and play music. There were chairs in rows where all the students, faculty and staff members, and people who wanted to attend Mass could sit on. In the middle, there was a space for everyone to walk to their seats, including altar servers and the priest to walk down the aisle to reach the table.

As usual, we all gathered together in the cafeteria where the chapel also was, sat down in our chairs, and began Mass. After communion ended, my mom walked up to the podium to speak to us about the Character Trait Award for the month. She told everyone I was the one receiving the award. I was in shock! I am not one to enjoy being the center of attention, and I remember feeling very embarrassed. In fact, my face started to turn red when everyone turned their heads to look in my direction. This particular day, I was wearing a cream-colored dress with a green sweater on top and black flats. I was shaking with nervousness when I heard my name called. As I walked up to the podium, I could feel my legs shaking and goosebumps forming as I went from hot to cold every few seconds. I walked up to the podium, gave a big smile, and then I spoke into the microphone thanking the people who voted for me for this virtue; I told them I was very honored to receive it. I then selected two people whom I thought best fit this category. The two students I selected walked up to the front where I was standing. Music then started to play as people started exiting the chapel and going back to their classes. My mom and the principal took out their cameras and got a photo of me and the students standing next to me. It was a very good day!

## CHAPTER NINE

# IT IS FINISHED!

———

This story is one that holds much significance. After her cancer treatment, my mom had started talking about retiring. She had put her heart and soul into this school and was ready to be finished with all the work she had put into it. She was very proud of the work she had started from the ground up to make this school the place not only what she wanted it to be, but also the place God wanted it to be.

My mom held a meeting for us, located in the conference room, telling us it was her last day at work because she was retiring. Everyone was very excited for her that she was getting to experience this next step in her life.

People asked her, "Marie, what are you going to do every day, now that you are retired?" My mom laughed, gave a smile, and replied, "I hope to play golf, travel, relax, and do anything I want."

Afterward, everyone stood up one by one and embraced her. My mom was very excited about this new journey she would be on after working on the school for as long as she did. She knew she had followed God's plan the way He wanted her to, as well as the way she wanted it. Everyone was very excited for her and this new season of life she would embark on.

When the meeting ended, my mom walked up to the front desk reception room to put letters in our mailboxes. These letters she wrote to us were thanking us for being a part of the school. The letter my mom wrote to me mentioned how grateful she was that she began the school for me. When reading the letter, I felt extremely sentimental and bittersweet. It was hard knowing this was her last day, but I also felt happy for her that she was making this decision. She left that day to start the next chapter in her life.

# EPILOGUE

In May 2017, a farewell Mass was held at Sophia Academy. In August 2017, Sophia Academy merged with Notre Dame Academy located in Duluth. Sophia Academy holds special memories in my heart and always will.

Melissa, my mom's assistant, mentioned, "Sophia Academy was an answer to many students' and parents' prayers. Students thrived there and would come back year after year after leaving to thank faculty and staff for helping them learn."

Anne, the Director of Liturgy, said, "Sophia Academy was a special place filled with special and unique students, an incredibly dedicated founder, faculty, and staff, and wonderful memories and stories. It was truly blessed by God! It was a blessing to so many students during almost two decades of educating both mind and soul!"

Made in the USA
Columbia, SC
20 October 2020